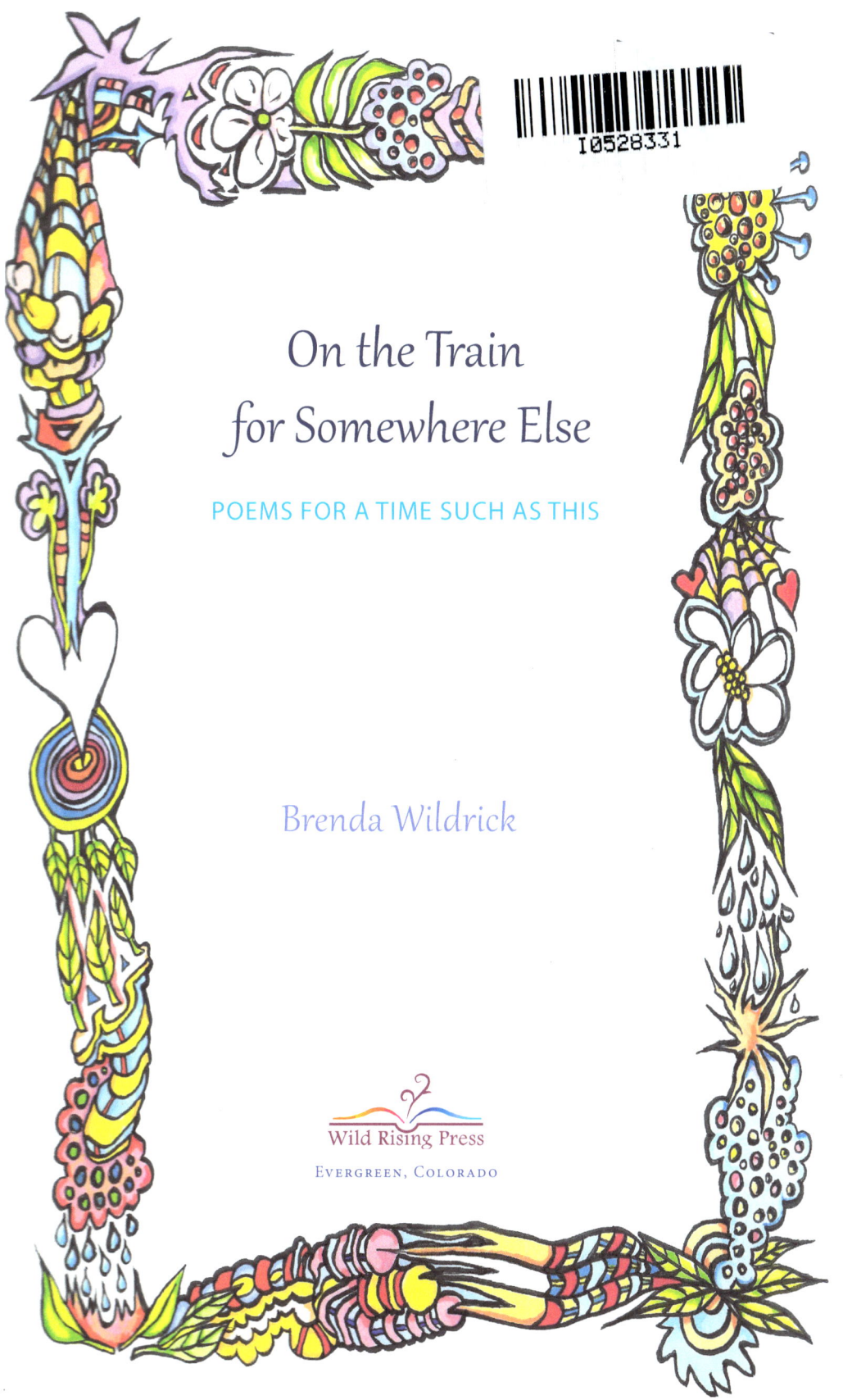

On the Train for Somewhere Else

POEMS FOR A TIME SUCH AS THIS

Brenda Wildrick

Wild Rising Press

EVERGREEN, COLORADO

Published by WILD RISING PRESS
Copyright ©2023 Brenda Wildrick.

Editor: Judyth Hill
Book & Cover Design: Mary M Meade
Cover & Interior Illustrations: Brenda Wildrick

wildrisingpress.com
ISBN 978-1-957468-15-0

To my husband, Kim, my daughters, Sharon and Shiloh,
and all my poetry community.

Contents

Part One

Healing Rain Against a Dark, Closed Window | 11

I Am Has Sent Me | 12

One Summer Night with a Wagon | 13

Open the Pearly Gates, Lord;
Daddy's on His Way | 14

Quieting My Agenda | 20

Two People Exit | 21

The Man in Chicago | 22

Forgotten Melody | 23

Waiting in Cardboard Castles | 24

Part Two

Sacred Stillness 29

Song of the Mountain 31

The Light Calls 33

Treasuring the Midnight Darkness 34

Day After Day in Tears and in Healing 35

In Living Colors of Death October Celebrates . 37

Ready to Embrace Winter 38

September, Just in Case 39

Part Three

A Time Such as This 43

April 2020 Haiku Collection 44

Children Take a Bow as the
Curtain Falls on 2021 46

Christmas Calls for Answers 47

How Can I Find Balance 48

In the Year of the Rat 49

Looking at Next Year's Calendar in 2021 . . . 51

Summer 2020 Finds the Courage to Explode . 52

A Cold Day in May 53

Broken House 54

Part Four

Christmas Lights Blinking in July 59

On the Train to Somewhere Else. 61

Spiders, Zombies, and Other

Dangerous Creatures. 63

To Protect the Innocent 66

Where His Journey Ended 67

On This Strange Stage 68

Blood Orange Poison and Bitter Memory. . . 70

The Book of John Mingles with News

(April 29th, 2023). 72

Acknowledgments *73*

Author's Biography *75*

Part 1

Healing Rain Against a Dark, Closed Window

The rain begins with sprinkles,
whispering to your dryness, whispering messages
you could not receive.
She loved you, Dear Friend, the best she could.
She was never enough to satisfy your needs,
never enough to meet your expectations,
never enough to undo the damage that she did.
She was proud of you, but that was not enough—
she could never tell you.

For you, she was inadequate.
By you, she was rejected.
Mourning some elusive sunshine, you never loved the rain.

You've built your anger into a fortress to protect you
from rain, from the simmering pain of abandonment.
Anger distracts you from taunting voices thundering
from both ends of that two-way street:
Not good enough! Never good enough!

The street is shining, slippery, wet,
healing rain is softly falling,
filling in empty spaces, with peace
melting down sharp edges. With acceptance

the rain restores your hope, washes away
fear that chokes the life from you.
Can you hear it
from somewhere behind your dark, closed window?

Take my hand. We'll step into the rain together.

I Am Has Sent Me

I am my daddy. I am a preacher too.
I am my childhood, full of church, Sunday School,
and Jesus Loves Me.
I am guilt, guilt and confusion tormenting my sleep.
I am peace like a river, God speaking peace to me at night.
I am learning to let guilt and confusion be,
to be gone, or to be quietly present.

I am climate change. I am forest fire.
I am a gentle snowflake, a thick wet blanket
of snow extinguishing wildfires.
I am the year that came in like a lamb, a lamb who
lay down with a lion, the prowling, roaring lion seeking
whom he may devour.
I am who set the horses free. I am who summoned
the four horsemen of the apocalypse.

I am divisiveness. I am healing.
I have come not to bring peace, but a sword.
A man's enemies will be the members
of his own household. Love your enemies.
Peace I give to you, not as the world gives.
Let not your heart be troubled, neither be afraid.
I am a resounding gong, a clanging cymbal. I am love.

I am becoming comfortable not fitting in. I am tired.
Come all you who are weary and I will give you rest.
I am peace like a river, I am Jesus loves me.
I am sharing peace with you, and with me, and with God.
What is your name, God?
I am who I am. Tell them I Am has sent you.

One Summer Night with a Wagon

We invented our own games, my cousins and I,
to play in our grandparents' backyard—
large, unfenced, beckoning.

One summer night, enveloped in soft warm darkness,
we had a wagon, a blanket, a flashlight—
what more could game-inventing
children need?

Two of us sat in the wagon, one holding the flashlight,
the blanket covering us both. Another cousin
pulled the wagon around the backyard.

Wheels bumped along over uneven ground,
fluttery butterflies in our tummies told
us the wagon could tip over at
any moment.

The flashlight's glow under the blanket was like captured stars.
The music of crickets and a distant
fading train whistle, our enchanted serenade.

Perhaps we also heard the cracking of tall wooden wheels slowly turning
behind horses, snorting, plodding down the rough-hewn trail,
pots and pans clanking off the side of the covered wagon,
rhythmic motion gently rocking a sleeping baby.

Perhaps we also heard silence, as we soared high above the earth
into the vast sprawling night sky, still sparkling with
limitless possibilities.

Open the Pearly Gates, Lord;
Daddy's on His Way

Talking was hard for Daddy since his stroke nearly three years before. So Daddy was quiet at the dining room table with his family and the hospice team—the chaplain, nurse, and social worker. I saw Daddy's expression change into something distant and sad when they started asking about funeral arrangements. Daddy wasn't dead. Next to him the chaplain, a tall African American woman with kind eyes and streaks of gray in her dark hair, asked him if he felt confident about his eternal destination. In that context, the question felt to me like just part of the routine, the routine with which Daddy was quietly irritated. But after a pause, he met her eyes, smiled slightly, and said "yes."

The chaplain herself was more subdued in a larger group. But Mom said, when it was just the three of them, she'd tell them stories about her childhood, how her mama used to make biscuits. The chaplain always called Daddy "pastor," because, like his own daddy, he had been a pastor, the shepherd of his flock, for many years. She would often burst into exuberant singing and powerful praying. And an expression would come across Daddy's face that looked like a grimace, showing all his broken and missing teeth. But it was actually a beautiful smile, and tears would run down his cheeks. "Getting blessed," he called it.

I think hospice workers must be angels somehow because what they do, coming alongside hurting families and gently guiding an individual through the transition from this life to the next, seems like too big a job for ordinary humans.

I saw the "getting blessed" expression one last time a couple of weeks later when Daddy couldn't get out of bed anymore and some people from church had gathered around to sing, pray, and read scripture. The next day he didn't open his eyes anymore, but all the grandchildren had arrived by then and we gathered around again and prayed, read to him, and sang hymns, including the one about the pearly gates, the song we used to sing together at the churches where Daddy was the pastor. Mom would play the piano and Daddy, my sisters, and I would sing. In 2004, we sang it again for the people who came for Mom and Dad's 50th anniversary celebration. It had been a spontaneous thing, not part of the planned event. Hey, look, a piano! Let's do our song! *He the pearly gates will open, so that I may enter in…*

The hospice nurses said Daddy could still hear us even when he couldn't respond anymore. The nurse who came that Sunday evening said we should call when Daddy passed, and the hospice people would take care of everything.

A few hours later, my sister made that call. And we sat together swaddled in soft conversation late at night, waiting.

Peace on Earth and Popcorn

December, 2016

They'd feed us peace
with our popcorn
if there was any money in it.

I sit in the dark composing myself—
although nearly everyone dies,
it wasn't a movie to cry for.

Eight more shopping days till Christmas.
Time is running out.
I hear the bells…
The old familiar carols play
There's still no peace on earth—I say.

The sky is brown in Texas today.
Leaves swirl,
we try to hold on to glass doors
at the mall.
Weather's changing,
galaxies at war,
crazy traffic this time of year.

In the dressing rooms,
we try on peace
but we already know—
it doesn't fit us.

My nephew in his Star Wars shirt,
Star Wars jacket, Star Wars pants,
would have worn the Star Wars socks
but they were in the wash.

Did you like the movie?

I see us—I don't say—
mingling with fanciful creatures from other planets.
I see beings in World War II uniforms and
Mideastern head coverings
and something about one of those fanciful
creatures tastes of Vietnam.

Where is that universal heart?
I see veins and arteries
intertwining through the throng
connecting, dividing
our cultures, our religions, our history.
It pulsates with blood and pain,
hate and terror,
camaraderie and courage,
and self-sacrifice
for a greater cause.

Yes—I say—it was a good movie.

The young ones talk of special effects
and comparisons with the others—
had to wait all those years for
technology to catch up with imagination.

They tell me the one we saw today
is a prequel to the original,
which I had seen nearly forty years ago
with a boy who would become my husband,
the first in a series.

Snow falls heavy in Colorado today,
as the day of reckoning dawns on America's
greatness. And a Russian ambassador lies
dead on the floor at an art exhibit in Turkey.

Rest in peace.
If life is war,
death must be peace—
it's only logical.

Remember Aleppo
Remember the Alamo
Remember 9-11
Never forget
Never forgive

Fear not, children,
we've no good news of peace on earth,
but still, we will bring you
great movies.

A unanimous gasp fizzles through the
sprawling theater.
The plug's been pulled
on the ever-increasing glaring lights
and blaring noise.
A fierce and frantic battle finally ends.
Did we win?

A great disturbance in the Force—
millions of voices,
and then one more,
suddenly silenced.

The crowd squirms and fidgets
in the unfamiliar quiet.

An ancient star and
an angel's voice
startle the darkness
that has not understood.
Angels sing out a message
of eternal peace, internal peace,
still ours for the receiving.

Princess Leia delivers the closing line.
The last word is hope.
We open it up
like a perfect gift.
Hope fits us.

Quieting My Agenda

I finally got him quieted.
He's sitting on a bench in the background,
I know you can still see him.

He is my agenda.
He is important. And valid. And urgent.
I call him "The Truth."

But, whenever you and I try to talk,
he keeps getting in the way.

I asked him to sit down and be quiet for now.
I'll bet you didn't think I could do it—
but I did. And I'm here. Fully present,

unaccompanied and unencumbered,
I hear you. I am listening.
What you have to say is important too.

My agenda has become quite vocal lately.
He doesn't always have the best manners,
but in this moment of distance, I realize—

I earn the right to be heard
by listening.

Two People Exit

Two people exit through tall glass doors.
Together they leave the old courthouse,
its stony walls blankly staring.

No sound, but nice dress shoes
tip tapping down
cold gray steps.

Final papers freshly signed.
A hug.
A tear—quickly wiped away.
No more words.

Two people turn,
and walk alone
toward separate vehicles.

The Man in Chicago

My grandmother told me,
told my sisters and cousins too—
as a reason to be quiet—
there's a man in Chicago
with a headache.

For years I saw him
in a dark Italian café,
head in his hands,
elbows on a small square table
with a red checked tablecloth
and a candle in a bottle,
wax dripping down.

Poor man—
suffering with the noise
of all those unruly children
miles away
in Colorado.

Forgotten Melody

Grandma has forgotten the melody.
Deep inside a purple flower she waits.
Sweetly she sings to a sleeping baby
but no bee is coming; it's too late.

Deep inside a purple flower she waits.
A grey-eyed cat wanders in and out
but no bee is coming; it's too late.
Holding tight to a rainbow trout—

a grey-eyed cat wanders in and out.
Grandma sits and rocks all day,
holding tight to a rainbow trout
but it's all staged; she's on display.

Grandma sits and rocks all day.
Waiting to be, waiting to live,
but it's all staged; she's on display.
And she has nothing more to give.

Waiting to be, waiting to live,
sweetly she sings to a sleeping baby.
And she has nothing more to give—
Grandma has forgotten the melody.

Waiting in Cardboard Castles

Opaque window to the depths of time
illuminates dust dancing over stacked boxes
like timid ghosts in the attic hidden.
Cardboard castles stuffed full of treasures.
Pearls of great price socked safely away
or worthless trash? How would I know?

Why are you taking up space? Do you know?
You once had purpose, in some forgotten time,
now wrapped and anonymously stashed away
in closets and basements. Towers of boxes
labeled only with beer names, buried treasures,
like unread books with wisdom hidden.

Fragile china adorned with gold, hidden
in newspapers from a world I'll never know,
waiting for a glorious special occasion. Treasures
suffocating under thick, heavy layers of time,
plotting escape, freedom from boxes—
delicate, admired, carried away,

to feed a family at formal table, not washed away,
but clinking with silverware, shine unhidden.
Mingling with polite conversation. No boxes
to dampen pleasant illusions. As if I know
all is well since we're not moving one more time.
Home feels real when we display our treasures,

like photos lamenting loved ones lost. Treasures
I can't replace—can't pretend they never went away—

I return to some remembered time,
erase regrets, redeem hastily hidden
failures. If only I might know
the secrets of the dusty boxes.

Pretty kitty, craving sparkle, fits into boxes,
springs free when she pleases, shredding treasures.
Nine lives of stark simplicity, little to know
or contemplate or find the space to put away.
Whiskers twitching, soft face mostly hidden.
Fearless kitty, fiercely guarding sacred time.

Boxes blaze or slowly rot away.
Treasures or trash—which have I hidden?
Someday I'll know. If I ever have time.

Part Two

Sacred Stillness

An old pickup truck rattles down a dirt road
and grinds to a stop somewhere in Wyoming.
It has landed, like a spaceship,
in a different world.

A girl, nearly grown, steps down
from the passenger seat.
She hears cattle softly lowing in the distance,
hears crickets
and the slamming of the pickup doors,
hears the crunch of gravel under her feet
and under the boots of the young cowboy.

In the silence that is not entirely silent,
she hears the absence of noise pollution,
sees the absence of light pollution
she has lived with all her life—
never noticing.

She experiences sacred stillness.
The depth and breadth and blackness
stretches far into eternity, darkness,
soft as kitten's fur. And pure,
even while not being entirely dark,
with the fading headlights,
the bright circle on the ground
from the flashlight.

And stars—billions and billions of stars—
tingling her skin
as she steps lightly down the Milky Way.

Song of the Mountain

A Golden Shovel after Isaiah 55:12-13a, NIV

I have come to the mountain to find you,
God. In reverent silence and in solitude I will
seek your face. Wild roses in my hair, I go
dancing toward a tumbling creek rushing out
to greet me. I hear your voice whispering in
cool pure water splashing my body with joy.
Slippery rocks tingle my delighted feet and
energize my being, reminding me to be.
Just be. Alive! God, I believe you have led
me here to drink in your essence as I go forth
into the presence of trees, branches in
formation, reaching up to pluck peace
from blue sky, a delicacy to satisfy the
hunger of one who dines with mountains.

Golden Eagles soar and call my name and
I answer their distant cry, while sacred hills
and hallowed ground hold fallen pines that will
nourish new life emerging, ready to burst
into butterfly color, ready to transform into
sweet aroma of undamaged nature. Song
of the mountain generously spreads before
me a banquet of questions. I dare to ask you,

God, will you allow us to destroy the earth? And
will unextinguishable fire consume us all?
Is that the unalterable destiny of all life, the
pristine waters, the eagles, the majestic trees?
To be charred to their bones? Will the future of

the planet be consumed, vanishing forever in the
depths of the hell man created? Wheat in the field
is burning. The poor will never eat of it. They will
starve, while some rich vile humans laugh and clap

for families shattered and homes destroyed. Their
greed wants only money and power. Their hands
drip with innocent blood. They lust for more instead
of permitting their eyes to flow with rivers of
compassion. God, if you forced us to reform, the
seeds of hate would sprout again like a thornbush.
We'd return like a dog to its vomit. Our own will
to change is our hope. Hope breathes and can grow.

We can listen to the voice of God in the
trickling creek, in the dry burning juniper,
in the tsunami, the flood, the drought,
in the hurricane and earthquake. But instead,
we blindly wait. It's too late. Unless enough of
us unite, take action, and rip out thorny briers
from our midst. We can choose to sow love into the
soil of our world; we can make space for the myrtle,
for the sunflower, for peace. If we will
water earth with our tears, hope may yet still grow.

The Light Calls

The light cannot be contained
The light cannot be controlled
The light will travel where it pleases
The light will not be imprisoned

Put it in a cage
it will shine through the bars
Put it under a shade
it will create dancing shadows

Come dance with the shadows—
the light calls

Be free
with me

Shine
with me

Illuminate
with me

Enlighten
with me

Be
with me

Together
we will warm
the winter world

Treasuring the Midnight Darkness

In the darkness
in the sleepless quiet
poetry books beckon me
to the lonely sitting room
tidy and never used
by anyone but me
and the cat with her soft fur
black and white
dark and light

She sits with me in the space
where I used to frantically
long for a quiet mind
and sleep

But I have come to value darkness
I have come to treasure my
midnight time
with poetry and silence
and sometimes a cat
for company

Day After Day in Tears and in Healing

I am Time, I am centuries ago. I am right now.
I turn a seed into a giant redwood, a 5,000-year-old
bristlecone pine, a young cornstalk,
its thick green leaves dancing with the wind, or
an apple tree laden with delicate pink blossoms.

I am weeks and months turning a fertilized egg,
ordinary, yet awe-inspiring in its completeness,
into a glorious eagle ascending into the heavens,
a noble lion, or a child, a cherished miracle.

I am there as a blank canvas becomes a priceless
work of art, and when piles, stacks, truckloads
of stones, bricks, glass, wood become a museum
or a place to worship. I am nine months expecting,
seasons of hope, waiting. I am a thousand years.

I am an hour, a few quick minutes. I am
a nanosecond, when hailstorms come,
when hurricanes, fires, earthquakes, bombs, bullets
blast from guns, their triggers pulled in malice,
carelessness, or despair. I am there in the tears,
in the wailing, in the deep grief.

I am the weeks and months
when helpers come bringing food and water.
I am there in the shouts of joy
as survivors are pulled from rubble.

I am the months and years of healing

and rebuilding as God and nature and humans
begin again. Willing. Even though
their deeply loved creations can still
be destroyed in a few seconds.

Day after day, century after century, I join God,
nature, and humans. We continue creating.

And beauty rises from ashes.

In Living Colors of Death October Celebrates

Jumbled pumpkins in big square bins
wait like kittens, hoping for a home.
Home. On the kitchen table.
Sharp knife pierces firm orange flesh.
Stringy slippery seedy slime. Splat.

Celebrate orange, golden, and red.
Sun shimmers in dying leaves,
in fading daylight.

Marigold in stiff petals
scatters her progeny.
October, you are no gentle caregiver,
your winds cover seeds haphazardly with dirt
and rain and snow and rotting foliage.
Celebrate, sleepy starts!

Ladies in black dresses,
high heels sink into soft black soil
beneath rich green grass
on the way to chairs under velvet canopy.
Celebrate a life
with green grass and black dresses
and nippy air just cool enough for a sweater.

Yellow blends calm with angry red
in flames that flicker
from October birthday candles,
from pumpkins'
eerie, crooked grins.

Ready to Embrace Winter

I am ready for you now, Winter.
Now that the dark has come and the cold
has come, I no longer dread you. Go ahead,
sting my skin and make me shiver.

I can't hibernate, can't hide from you.
I will go for brisk walks, drink steaming tea.
I will find a campfire and stand close to loved ones,
share a blanket, and sing all the old Christmas
carols even if we've forgotten the words and never could
do much more than make a joyful noise.

We will sing with the crackling fire
and let smoke follow us.
Watch the sparks rise to meet the stars,
search for constellations,
whisper love poems to a moon
surrounded by a halo of shadows.

September, Just in Case

Late September allows no assumptions.
It might be fiery hot like the color of maple leaves,
or it might be icy, coaxing out goose bumps
through thin summer clothing.
There might be torrential rains, sudden flooding,
soft snowflakes falling on crunchy ground
or melting in the air.

One September, years ago,
doomsday prophets
predicted a catastrophic event—
saying a third of all earth would burn
after the 4th blood moon.

I don't let my heart dwell on such things.
But, just in case, I spend my Septembers
watching aspen leaves turn golden,
picking brilliant red tomatoes from between the
brown dead leaves in the garden,

spinning a silky cocoon of poetry around myself.
I know the poetry cocoon can't protect me,
but it lets me guzzle the last delicious swallows of
September joy from this life.
Just in case…

Part Three

A Time Such as This

The wind whispers through locked doors.
We are dust collecting,
coloring outside lines,
drawing circles around language,
language that has seen,
but has not believed.

We speak of earthly things,
we speak the words of God.
We are losing what we thought we knew
but we will collect the fragments
and nothing will be wasted.

The sea has been stirred up,
the sky has already grown dark
but we belong to these days.
We have been born for a time
such as this.

Peace be with you
and
do not be afraid.

April 2020 Haiku Collection

Be gone, Corona.
In the midst of it, Spring. This
Bud's for you. Drink up.

A man wears a red
bandanna. He might shop
or rob a stagecoach.

Innocent sentenced
to death gasping for last breath
with no fair trial.

Donald, Doctor F,
terrible reporters. Great
job, All! Confusion.

Skies are blue. Frantic
pace slows. Are we ready to
go back to normal?

Covid positive
people in public buildings
coughing. No safety.

As April begins,
we strain to hear faint cries of
newborn miracles.

April morning. Scrape
iced car. Grateful mental health
work is essential.

April Sunday. Life
blooms, sun caresses, birds sing.
Sermon live-streamed. Blessed.

Children Take a Bow as the Curtain Falls on 2021

White fire rains down, drowns an innocent voice.
Toy soldiers armed with plastic guns stand by.
Protesters with signs shout for life or choice,
we asked for new normal but got no reply.

Toy soldiers armed with plastic guns stand by.
Dad stabs babies, saves world from serpent DNA—
we asked for new normal but got no reply.
Cute clothes, matching mask, school's first day,

Dad stabs babies, saves world from serpent DNA.
Blood dries slowly in the halls we've left behind.
Cute clothes, matching mask, school's first day,
children make weapons from anything they find.

Blood dries slowly in the halls we've left behind.
Mom wears a torn Christmas sweater and rocks.
Children make weapons from anything they find.
Bullets stop the ticking of the classroom clocks.

Mom wears a torn Christmas sweater and rocks.
Protesters with signs shout for life or choice.
Bullets stop the ticking of the classroom clocks.
White fire rains down, drowns an innocent voice.

Christmas Calls for Answers

Can we find peace or hearts that are willing?
What has this year unleashed upon the world?
Why so much stealing, destroying, and killing?
Beauty lies in ruins as destruction is hurled.

What has this year unleashed upon the world?
Blood soaks the ground like a stagnant river,
beauty lies in ruins as destruction is hurled—
huddled in basements wrapped up in shiver.

Blood soaks the ground like a stagnant river.
For the next missile strike silent children wait
huddled in basements wrapped up in shiver.
Will anyone survive in the land of too late?

For the next missile strike silent children wait.
Can angels break darkness to sing, "fear not"?
Will anyone survive in the land of too late?
Can Christmas sneak into a year that joy forgot?

Can angels break darkness to sing, "fear not"?
Why so much stealing, destroying, and killing?
Can Christmas sneak into a year that joy forgot?
Can we find peace or hearts that are willing?

How Can I Find Balance

How can I stay upright
when the world is tilting sideways,
on the verge of spilling its contents
like grape juice spilling onto new carpet...

I used to think about grape juice.
I used to worry about nice things getting ruined,
but now the world is tilting sideways,
spilling blood.

I don't know how much blood
will spill on our pretty future.

Before the war,
despite global pandemic,
horrendous wildfires, devastating storms,
my hope for the future still held tight to the last,
a chunk of free-floating optimism, bobbing
like an ice cube...melting.

In the Year of the Rat

January watches China, far in the distance.
Year of the Rat hijacked by a bat. Breathe
easy. That virus can't threaten our home.
Trending impeachment, war with Iran? Mask
the truth. No cause for concern—we hope.
Only one case in the USA. All is normal.

February leaps, as flames lick last drops of normal.
We assume the virus will stay in the distance,
with chronic war, crushing poverty, shattered hope
that defile lands outside privileged air we breathe.
Election chugs like a train on track, mass shooter's mask
hides a white face. Virus toll 68, inching closer to home.

March is a lamb, gently breezing our beloved home.
Brave trees bud, dodging usual late blizzards. Normal
this time of year. Sudden! State of emergency! Mask
your shock! No toilet paper, no food in stores. Distance
yourselves! Shut everything down! Stop! Breathe!
100,000 may die. But spring feels a little like hope.

April adjusts to isolation, flattens the curve…kind of hope.
Online school, live-streamed church, work from home.
Economy crashes. Wait for stimulus pay. Some still breathe;
some do not. In two weeks, we'll be back to normal.
Task force chats. Conspiracies. Unemployment. Social distance:
six feet. Red bandanna, cheery flowers—make your own mask.

May heats divisive politics. Defy the orders. Ditch the mask.
Naked face is new MAGA cap. Enemies desist! God's our hope.

Reached the goal—100,000. Open up. Keep your distance
and wash your hands. An old woman dies in a nursing home.
Old man in a hospital cries alone. Embrace our new normal.
In the street, black man dies. We all hear—*I can't breathe.*

June forgets Pandemic. Protesters, police, rioters breathe
in fire and smoke. Revolution! Politics explode! Mask
abandoned. Virus is still killing thousands. That's normal.
Grief deepens, gulf widens. But some start to listen. Hope
feels possible. But lies twist into the braid of truth. Home
cries with Tulsa. Heal the bleeding gash. Bridge the distance.

Breathe deeply, dear heroes. Inhale fresh hope.
Throw off the mask and go home
while normal self-destructs in the distance.

Looking at Next Year's Calendar in 2021

2022 bleeds on calendar's glossy pages.
Stone chickens watch from roof and sky.
Cackling warns of storms as terror rages,
I wave my handkerchief, say good-bye.

Stone chickens watch from roof and sky.
Men in moonlight play a tune so solemn,
I wave my handkerchief, say good-bye.
Yellow trees predict an ordinary autumn.

Men in moonlight play a tune so solemn,
as if seeing the future, my heart grieves.
Yellow trees predict an ordinary autumn,
I hear a mournful whisper in the leaves.

As if seeing the future, my heart grieves.
Hope and optimism struggle to survive.
I hear a mournful whisper in the leaves,
I tune out harsh noise and remain alive.

Hope and optimism struggle to survive.
Cackling warns of storms as terror rages.
I tune out harsh noise and remain alive.
2022 bleeds on calendar's glossy pages.

Summer 2020 Finds the Courage to Explode

I want to break through the silence.
I want to silence the fear.
I want to fear my hesitation
more than I fear disapproval.
I want to frown disapprovingly
upon my need for perfection.
I want to perfect my courage.
I want to encourage my hidden self.

I want my courage to explode
like boxes of improperly stored chemicals
cackling among themselves, waiting for a spark.
I want to be the spark.

I want to spark the dialogue.
I want dialogue to smash rusted padlocks
off ears that have long ago forgotten how to listen.

I want listening to become a sweet mama softly
singing to the screaming in our city streets.
I want to bravely peer out my open window to see
anger wiping tears from its red, wet face,
see its heaving chest, hear its shallow gasps for breath slowing,
as it settles into peaceful sleep,

satisfied,
it has finally been heard.

A Cold Day in May

May is allowed cold days
within the quotation marks of normal.

May is diversity of weather,
Spring is diversity of thought.

I want to think of Spring for
a moment. Instead of war.
But when I try to think of Spring,
I remember that green is no longer
innocent and growing and hopeful—

green is the blending, the crushing,
of blue and yellow.

Green is the color heroes wear
when they defend the children,
lives shattered in the deafening
sounds of explosions and sirens.

Green is the color enemies wear
when they destroy the children,
stealing their innocence
in clouds of black smoke and the
stench of living things burning.

Watching from a safe distance,
I walk with a limp today. I endure my
insignificant pain, knowing it will
fade when the weather smiles,
knowing tomorrow will be
a warmer May Day.

Broken House

Therefore everyone who hears these words of mine and puts them
into practice is like a wise man who built his house on the rock.
The rain came down, the streams rose,
and the winds blew and beat against that house;
yet it did not fall, because it had its foundation on the rock. |
—Mathew 7:24-25

The words of the rock foundation were many,
words like "love" and "forgive" and "have faith"
and "do not worry" and "ask, seek, and knock"
and "produce good fruit."

Our house is divided against itself,
barely standing.
Our house is battered,
severely damaged by storms,
ready to fall with a great crash.

I had searched for common ground,
and I found it beneath our divided house.
Our common ground is made of fear,
of worry, of arrogance,
and of putting our hope in only ourselves.

But our common ground is sand.
Our broken house is built on sand.

My heart too is broken,
broken for countries and people far away.
Broken pieces have pierced my blessing bubble.

And even gratitude feels hollow, selfish
as I lie awake in my warm bed,
digesting our Thanksgiving feast.

I wonder why I should be so blessed
while others suffer.
I wonder if my tears,
my dollars given, my prayers
matter.

Our house is broken,
and must be fixed.
And our foundation remade:
the sand fused to rock—
rocks of "love," "forgive" and "have faith."

Come, let us join hands,
All who are broken
All who are willing
All who are brave…

Together we will find our way.
Together, rebuild our foundation.

Part Four

Christmas Lights Blinking in July

Things fell apart after Dad left. First it was the car, which had seemed just fine the day before. But when Dad left, the car Mother drove began dropping its shiny metal parts, leaving them along the road like Hansel and Gretel's breadcrumbs. I followed them on my bicycle when I rode home from school. But it wasn't a good day to come home. The roof had begun dropping shingles and nails and even wood beams so fast I barely escaped getting bonked on my head. I don't know why I dared to go inside, because chunks of the ceiling had already landed in messy chalky piles on the carpet, and they were still falling. In the kitchen, the appliances rumbled threateningly, and the doors and knobs popped off, crashing into each other as they flew across the room.

I hoped Mother was still in one piece, but I couldn't find her. I tried to call Dad, but the phone crumbled in my hand. All I could do was scream and run…

Rounding the corner, I see lights from the soft wet corners of my eye. Corners do not belong in eyes. And Christmas lights do not belong on my house, in July. I move in closer to get a better look. Blinking off and on—the lights are doing it and my eyes are doing it. Blinking, blinking, blinking. Mesmerized, I step up onto the front porch and reach for the lights. Like a mist, I drift through the wall, not as solid as one might expect. The whole wall is made of lights, lights that blink and draw me in. I enter into a magical place where there is no darkness and no winter. The weather is perfect and doesn't feel like either July or December.

Wrapped in lights like a sparkling Christmas tree, I drift. I am a cloud, soft and billowy and free and floating through a sky that can't be real. I don't want to let it disappear by opening my eyes to reality. Blinking, blinking, keep on blinking…

How long can I keep blinking? Blinking back tears, I hear a soft sweet voice. *Let the tears flow,* the voice says. *Let them be your liquid courage,* she says, and she is my mother. Our tears splash together.

He's not coming back, is he? I ask, as the flow of our tears slows to a trickle.

No, she says, *he is not. And no, your dad's leaving was not your fault. And no, things will not be the same. And no, we are not alone; do you see the angels?*

Come help me, she says. And together we wad up the "no's" like paper to be thrown away.

Now, she says—*We are ready for the "yes's."*

Yes—I say—*I see the angels.*

Yes—she says—*we will pick up the pieces.*

Yes—she says—*we will heal.*

On the Train to Somewhere Else

I hate it here! she says again.
Her mama sighs.

I'm going somewhere else.
She's 17.

Her mama sighs
and tries not to worry.

She remembers moving to this quiet town—
her child didn't think it so dull
when she was four and everything was new
and fresh and delightful and she felt a little
frightened of the mournful, rumbling, fading sounds
of trains, going somewhere else.

I hate these trains,
and I hate these cows and I hate these cornfields.
Her mama remembers those words
and the note on the bed, and the quiet.

Nothing left now but the quiet.

And she is 17
when she walks to the dark abandoned
train station and stands before the door.
Heavy door covered in dust and rust and memories
and fingerprints of ordinary people
who have touched the door, pulled it open.

Creaking heavy dusty rusty door opens slowly,

light tempts her sleepy eager eyes.

She hears a voice saying—*Come on in.*
She steps up onto the wooden floor, clean and polished.

She hears the clicking, thudding noise of many feet.

She sees funny shoes with buttons
and women in long dark dusty skirts.
She sees men in wool coats with long rows of buttons.
Why so many buttons? she wonders.

She bathes in warm greetings
and doesn't pause to consider why
they don't seem to notice she isn't dressed like them.

Where are you going? a man asks.
Do you have a ticket?
The girl pauses, doesn't know what to say.
I just want to go somewhere else, she answers.

You're right on time.
The train for somewhere else approaches now.
The girl hears the whistle, haunting, growing louder.
Black smoke billows,
bright light beckons.

So excited, so intrigued
She forgets to ask,
Is this a one-way trip?

Spiders, Zombies, and Other Dangerous Creatures

In speaking of spiders, spiders and snakes,
of dogs and roses, of humans of all kinds,
of swine in their pearls,
and silk purses made of sow's ears.
Of all such creatures, great and small,
one can only say they will be true to their nature.

One might manage them and nurture them,
love them and hate them,
cage them and embrace them,
avoid them, kill them,
reject them and accept them
just the way they are.
But can they, or will they, all be changed?

Attacking out of somewhere deep within
their own damage or their own nature,
they seek only self-preservation.
Sorry. No offense. No harm intended.

Most are intentionally oblivious,
though many put good effort
into the trampling under foot,
and a few aggressively seek peace.

Lions eagerly lie down with lambs,
though swords resist becoming plowshares
(having been told they are less mighty than pens)
they jealously, violently seek to disprove their impotence.

Fears take shape, becoming imaginary undead creatures
of exaggerated power and horror,
biting and devouring with gore and graphic detail.
Chills and thrills for entertainment
and whispered reassurance—
it isn't real!

While real threats too ominous to be ignored
are quite gracefully ignored, nonetheless

good and evil blend and merge into a dangerous thing
of color and beauty,
becoming a speck or a plank in the eye of the beholder.

Big Brother is watching you, is watching us all
as the future fades far into the distant past.

The blind lead the blind down the broad road
that leads to destruction,
and babies take candy from strangers. Easily

the blood of innocents cries out, while some survivors,
having never been shown the better way,
do unto others as was done unto them.

A multitude of sins covers over love,
while a kernel of truth falls into a pile of old cliches,
Biblical and literary references irrelevant to many.

But when the kernel of truth dies, it may still produce a crop,
thirty or sixty or a hundred times what was sown.

Trappings of a culture that many have discarded
go unrecognized,

as the young ones seek a better path—
which they might find.

Or they might find something far worse.
Or the path may come full circle,
returning back again
to its beginning.

It is what it is—the people say,
which is a most excellent answer,
being as it is a bit of wisdom which says nothing,
while at the same time—

says it all.

To Protect the Innocent

When the names were changed to protect
the innocent, the innocent wore their new names
proudly like designer labels. They carefully snuck
unnoticed into movies. They became actors,
becoming someone else, wearing a new name,
then throwing it off, discarding it
like a worn-out garment.

Then the innocent walked about naked, having
forgotten who they were, who they used
to be, and who they had long ago hoped
to become. They wandered into a large
pool of water and hid themselves,
but they were not lost.

They began to call out to each other. They called
one Petrichor and another Wildflower. Others
were called Brainstorm, Awakening,
Rebirth.

They stepped out of the pool glowing
and dripping, but clothed with springtime,
energy, and new purpose.

Where His Journey Ended

They found him.
It was a miracle—
like sunshine permeating
the steel of false hope
or the ragged whimpers
of reluctant locomotives.

They found him,
far away across the sea
long after they had
given up searching.

Get into the boat,
they implored.
Surely you must
be hungry.
But he shook his head
and would not come along.

They found him—
but they wouldn't understand,
and he could not explain.

He didn't know where he had gone,
or why his journey had ended,
he only knew—
in all the years he'd been alive,
he'd never felt less lost.

On This Strange Stage

It began badly—
with a falling star landing
on a frozen lake, its five points
struck and stuck through the ice.

The sharp ends attracted fish
who nibbled and nibbled
until their insides glowed
like fool's gold laughing.

We've come through fire—
the glowing fish gurgled.
*We will erupt like an ancient
volcano with lava flowing,
thick like sticky hot fudge*

*and lumpy with rocks and houses
and trees and dead things,
their faces contorted in screams,
still flowing with the lava
like drowning things bobbing
in rushing water of a stream
in flood stage.*

Are we humans there yet? Or here—
on this strange stage,
our feathers dipped in indigo
ink, ready to write an ending
to the world's tragic story.

Call me a princess.
Call me a frog.
We are dancing
on enemy soil
while yellow-eyed wolves
crouch between the charred remains
of giant redwood trunks

clinging to the edge of time
clinging by a single
unraveling root.

Blood Orange Poison and Bitter Memory

I am a healing raindrop dancing lightly
over deeply buried graves of forgotten nights,
full of uncomforted sobbing.
I am not quite free.

You are a silver salmon struggling against
the current, against grizzly bears,
against fishermen, fighting
with all your strength, never expecting to survive.

I am a lost refugee, eyes brimming with unspilled
tears, scanning bleak deserts for an elusive mirage.
I am an ocean of passionate fantasy.
I am not quite drowning.

You are my explanation, my exclamation mark,
shifting, skirting, sputtering,
to make my sentence stop.

I am thunder cracking, not quite loud enough,
lightning flashing, not quite bright enough
to reach the winter moon.

You are a falling star nobody notices,
absorbing the disillusionment of all ungranted wishes.
You are the Big Dipper dripping with rich red wine,
infused with blood orange poison and bitter memory.

I am emerging from a torn pocket,
escaping coarse cruel sandpaper
scraping and smoothing me smaller.

You are relentlessly seeking the black-iced highway
where our shattered, mismatched hearts collide,
screeching, screaming, gasoline leaking onto pavement,
20-foot flames licking the sky, thick black burnt muffins
of smoke, acrid stench of toxic misunderstood words.

I am a red glowing ember, warm.
A quieting, settling fireplace fire,
I am not quite extinguished.

The Book of John Mingles with News (April 29th, 2023)

We were going in and out searching for pasture,
but our passports were locked in abandoned embassies.
We tried to get into boats and cross the sea,
but online racists were stealing military secrets.
They were climbing over elsewhere
as a deadly fungus quietly spread across America.
Listen, believe. This will shock you.
You need to shut the *you know what* up and step back.
I don't recognize the voice of strangers
in drone strikes or on Hunter Biden's laptop.

We received only one boat.
Will that be enough
as we navigate the debt ceiling
and accomplish the works of God?
Even though we were presumed dead for decades,
the bread came down from heaven.
Even though a man killed five neighbors after one
asked him to stop shooting in his yard.

We will never hunger, never thirst.
There is reason to hope—
in abundance of life
as bombs fall and bullets blast
and our hearts are broken within us.

We will find our way to the gate.

Acknowledgments

Sending much gratitude to Judyth Hill for mentoring, inspiring, editing, and pulling together all the pieces involved in this creation. Much gratitude to Mary Meade for encouragement and expertise in designing my book and including my artwork for the cover and section openings. And to Mary and Judyth collectively, as Wild Rising Press, for publishing my book.

Thank you to Rachel Kellum for early inspiration and for introducing me to Columbine Poets of Colorado. I am grateful as well to Valerie Szarek, Rosemerry Wahtola Trommer, Julie Cummings, Anita Jepson-Gilbert, and all the talented poets I have come to know and admire through Columbine and other groups. Thanks for teaching me so much through your awesome workshops and input on my writings.

Thanks also to Jon Sebba for helping with some of my poems and for introducing me to the Arizona State Poetry Society. And much gratitude to Jon Erikson and others for joining us over the years for our local Tumbleweed poetry group.

Also sending much gratitude to my husband, Kim, for his patience and for going with me to many poetry events, and also to him and to my daughters, my mom, and other family members for listening to my poems in progress.

In memory of Bill Reed, who was my first muse and inspiration, who got me started writing poetry and who gave me my first set of felt-tipped markers. I could never have imagined how I would love using markers for my artwork!

Author's Biography

 Brenda Wildrick, poet, active member of Columbine Poets of Colorado and the Arizona State Poetry Society, has won contests sponsored by each of these societies. Her work has appeared in a Columbine Poets anthology, and she will have a poem included in the 2023 anthology.

She had a winning poem published in the Arizona Poetry Society's 2022 *Sandcutters* anthology and will have several more winning poems included in the 2023 *Sandcutters* anthology.

Wildrick has shared over 100 poems, stories, and drawings on Scribd.com and has been leading the Tumbleweeds poetry group in her hometown since 2011. Wildrick frequently reads her work at open mics. This is her first book.

Luminari, the calligraphic brainchild of Philip
Bouwsma, and employed for the section open-
ers herein, is a deep and fitting partnership for
this collection of inspirited poems. Luminari
is a typographical mirror of High Middle Ages
liturgical writing; Its capital letters, influenced
by famous twelfth century psalters, echoes the
subliminal sense of prayerful attention in the
poems. Gabriola, John Hudson's lively type-
face seen in the poem's titles, was inspired by
an idea from music: that the same melody can
be played in multiple modes and is consonant
with the way each poem sinuously develops
and shifts within a theme.

Adobe Garamond, utilized for the body text
of the poems, is a digital re-enlivening of the
renowned sixteenth century fonts of Claude
Garamond, meticulously designed to resem-
ble legible pen-and-ink handwriting. This font
lends the poems a sense of delicate immedi-
acy—and offers the reader that final flavor of
grace intended by the poet.

www.ingramcontent.com/pod-product-compliance
Lightning Source LLC
Chambersburg PA
CBHW040848120626

46547CB00001B/71